Playmakers

Strikers

Lynn M. Stone

Rourke
Publishing LLC
Vero Beach, Florida 32964

www.rourkepublishing.com

PHOTO CREDITS: All photos © Lynn M. Stone

Editor: Robert Stengard-Olliges

Cover and page design by Tara Raymo

Library of Congress Cataloging-in-Publication Data

Stone, Lynn M.
 Strikers / Lynn Stone.
    p. cm. -- (Playmakers)
 ISBN 978-1-60044-598-9
 1. Soccer--Juvenile literature. I. Title.
 GV943.25.S86 2008
  796.334--dc22
                                        2007019515

Printed in the USA

CG/CG

Rourke Publishing

www.rourkepublishing.com – rourke@rourkepublishing.com
Post Office Box 3328, Vero Beach, FL 32964

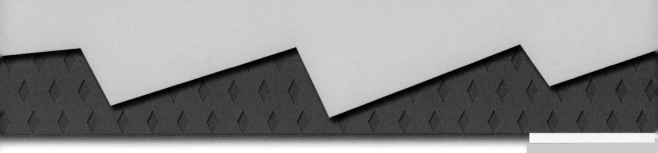

Table of Contents

The Striker

The striker on a soccer team typically plays a forward position from which to **attack** the opponent's goal. When a team lines up on the field, the striker, or strikers, line up closest to the opposing goal. Strikers are also known as forwards, attackers, and front-runners. The position is basically an **offensive**—or attack—position. A one-striker in a two-striker offense may often have to retreat to a backfield defense. Strikers also shift into defense when opposing defenders try to start an attack of their own.

The striker keeps the ball moving forward, toward the opponents' goal.

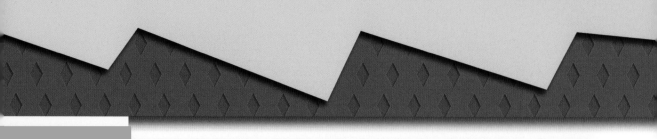

On the attack, forwards race downfield.

Modern soccer teams play from many **formations**. The role of the striker changes from one formation and game to another. Any player, except for the goalkeeper, could be a striker. Even an outside **back**, a defensive player, could rush forward into an attack position. In most situations, however, the strikers—if a team uses more than one—are the front forwards. The center forward is typically the striker in a one-striker offense.

Strikers are generally the players most likely to score goals, and they are the players expected by the team to score goals. **Midfielders** of the attacking team typically try to pass the ball to a striker.

Using her head to control the ball, a striker drives home a practice goal.

A midfielder corrals a ball before looking to pass.

In real game situations, most soccer teams use one or two forwards because other players also get into the attack. While a team may list three starting "forwards," the likelihood of three players as true forwards is small. A team can't afford to have three players locked into the forward line. That would expose the team's rear-guard defense to the opposing team's attack.

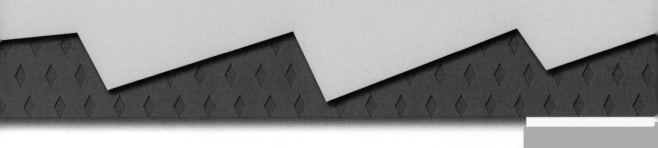

Forwards need to pass the ball in addition to kicking on-goal or dribbling.

The Striker's Skills

A striker is a model of **athleticism**. Part of the athleticism involves speed and great eye-foot **coordination**. A striker needs to be able to kick a soccer ball quickly, cleanly, and with either foot. Some players kick a ball harder than others. Velocity can be useful if it is accomplished with accuracy. A good striker must be able to change speed as the situation demands.

A forward (left) shows great eye-foot coordination in keeping the ball away from the defender (right).

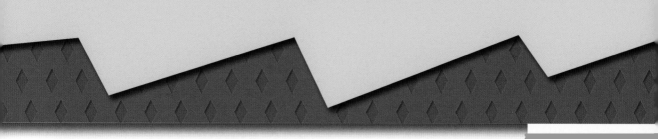

A powerful, booming kick is an asset if it can be done accurately.

A striker tends to be a skillful player "in the air." Many soccer goals are scored not by a kick, but by a player "heading" a ball into the net. A skilled player can whip a soccer ball off his or her head with velocity and accuracy! The most athletic players can leap high into the air to head a ball.

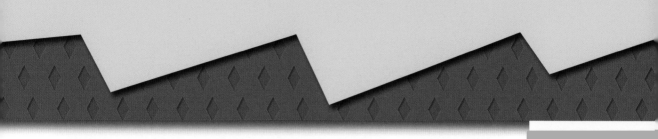

Playing the game "in the air" can lead to dramatic, headed goals.

A striker's skills go well beyond being athletic. Being smart and composed are necessary assets. Composure involves being cool in a pressure-filled situation. A striker has to be able to react to the pressure around him or her and at the same time recognize opportunity when it comes. A striker has to make quick, smart decisions. Knowing when to pass or dribble, and when to attack the goal with a kick.

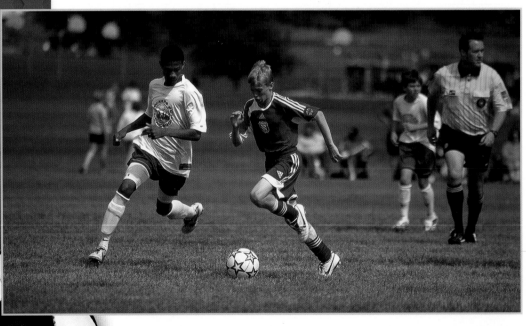

Faced with an onrushing defender, a forward (right) will have to make a quick decision—keep the dribble or pass.

Part of a striker's skill is in knowing how hard to kick the ball to put a shot past the goal keeper.

So, You Want to Be a Striker?

The striker role requires leadership and the ability to take charge, even if the striker's decisions are not widely popular. As one coach said, "Someone has to decide 'I can do it!'"

Strikers should have a take-charge attitude.

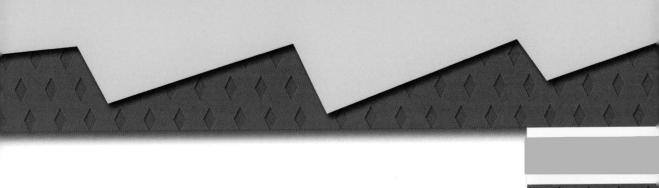

Heading a soccer ball requires concentration and coordination.

Running speed is a great asset for a striker.

Striker positions require speed. You don't necessarily have to be the fastest member of the team, but you can't be the slowest either. A benefit for a team with an extremely fast striker is that it may get away with using just one striker because that player can cover so much ground by him or herself.

Foot skills are extremely important for a striker.

You don't have to be big to be a striker, but a tall, strong player with the same skills as a smaller player is an advantage. The larger player will be less likely to be knocked off a contested ball.

The "knock" on big strikers used to be their lack of foot skills. Many of today's big players have foot skills that rival those of their smaller teammates.

Like all players, strikers find that soccer is often a game of contact.

Glossary

athleticism (ath LET uh siz uhm) – the ability to be athletic, highly coordinated, agile

attack (uh TAK) – to move forward in an organized way toward the opponent's goal

back (BAK) – a largely defensive soccer player who is generally "back," close to his or her team's goal

coordination (koh OR duh na shuhn) – the ability to easily and accurately control one's hand and foot movements in the context of a given sport

formations (for MAY shuhnz) – the organized ways in which soccer teams use their players in both offensive and defensive situations

midfielder (mid FEEL dur) – the player who tends to operate in the middle part of a soccer field and become involved with both offense and defense

offensive (uh FEN siv) – referring to a team with possession of the ball and moving toward the opponent's goal

Index

Further Reading

Crisfield, Deborah. *The Everything Kids' Soccer Book*. Adams Media, 2002.
DK Publishing Staff. *Soccer*. DK Publishing, 2005.
Gifford, Clive. *Soccer Skills*. Houghton Mifflin, 2005.

Website to Visit

http://expertfootball.com/gossip/answer.php?qid=238
http://www.soyouwanna.com/site/minis/mini/soccermini/soccermini4.html
http://expertfootball.com/coaching/positions.php

About the Author

Lynn M. Stone is the author of more than 400 children's books. He is a talented natural history photographer as well. Lynn, a former teacher, travels worldwide to photograph wildlife in its natural habitat.